AF885398

Denied U.S. Immigration?

Your Attorney Can Challenge The Decision
And Help You Achieve Your Lifelong Goals

Patrick Long, Esq.

Copyright © 2022 by Patrick Long, Esq.

All rights reserved. No part of this publication may be reproduced, distributed, or transmitted in any form or by any means, including photocopying, recording, or other electronic or mechanical methods, without the prior written permission of the publisher, except in the case of brief quotations embodied in critical reviews and certain other noncommercial uses permitted by copyright law. For permission requests, write to the publisher, addressed "Attention: Permissions Coordinator," at the address below.

Jacobs & Whitehall
21750 Hardy Oak Blvd
Suite 104
#51700
San Antonio, Texas 78258
www.jacobsandwhitehall.com

Ordering Information:

Quantity sales. Special discounts are available on quantity purchases by corporations, associations, and others. For details, contact the publisher at the address above.

Orders by U.S. trade bookstores and wholesalers. Please contact Jacobs & Whitehall: Tel: (888) 991-2766 or visit www.jacobsandwhitehall.com.

Printed in the United States of America

Published in 2022

ISBN: 978-1-954506-73-2

DISCLAIMER

This publication is intended to be used for educational purposes only. No legal advice is being given, and no attorney-client relationship is intended to be created by reading this material. The author assumes no liability for any errors or omissions or for how this book or its contents are used or interpreted, or for any consequences resulting directly or indirectly from the use of this book. For legal or any other advice, please consult an experienced attorney or the appropriate expert, who is aware of the specific facts of your case and is knowledgeable in the law in your jurisdiction.

Patrick Long Law Firm, PC
1452 Dorchester Avenue
Floor 4
Dorchester, MA 02122
(617) 718-5550
www.patricklonglaw.com

Testimonials

"Patrick was amazing, he made sure all my questions were answered. Even though I was very young, he treated me with respect and made sure I understood the process. I would definitely recommend him."

– Karen S.

****

"Mr. Long is very honest and he responds to our immigration issues/questions promptly. He is helping me with an immigration case and keeps us informed about our case. I highly recommend Mr. Patrick Law Firm."

– Emad M.

****

"He helped me deal with various Immigration issues. His professional experience and well-developed knowledge of Immigration has solved my problems."

– A Satisfied Client

****

"I felt comfortable with that decision! My family has been grateful because Patrick has traced to help us get a good possibility for our case!"

– Oneyda S.

****

"I was treated with respect, answered all my questions, kept up to date with my case, and I felt comfortable discussing my case with him, he came highly recommended and he showed for it. He is professional and informed, I will totally recommend him."

– Chikeluba A.

****

"Attorney Patrick Long treated me well; with respect and understanding. I feel happy that I decided to hire Atty. Long. I've already recommended Attorney Long to many of my friends and family members."

– Joseph P.

****

TABLE OF CONTENTS

About The Author

I grew up in Knoxville, Tennessee. I left home and moved to Massachusetts, alone, at 16 so I could start college early. I attended Simon's Rock College, got a master's degree at what is now the University of New Hampshire Law School, and then went to Suffolk University for law school. When I finished law school, I knew I wanted to make a difference in the world but didn't know how yet. A friend who was obsessed with immigration law asked me to work on some cases with her, and it opened my eyes.

Growing up, all the way through law school, I had heard about all the injustices in the criminal justice system and knew that was something I was interested in. But immigration is 100x more unfair, and the government keeps that a secret. In immigration court, you don't have most of the rights you'd have in a real court.

You can be held in jail as long as your case takes, sometimes for many years, and the burden of proof is on you to prove you aren't dangerous. The government can use whatever hearsay accusations or speculation it wants, with no proof. There is no jury. There is no right to remain silent, no presumption of innocence. The law is so complicated that even most lawyers don't understand it. You have to navigate this alone, or with the attorney you hire (don't count on a free attorney if you can't afford one; those don't exist in immigration). And all of this exists just to punish you for being born in the wrong place!

When I learned all of this, I wanted to do my part to fix it. So I practice primarily immigration law, combined with some criminal and family law, which I think it's important to keep current on in order to know how to solve every immigration problem that comes to me. Sometimes the remedy to your problem lies somewhere outside the immigration system.

Guiding Clients In Challenging Immigration Rulings

I have been practicing since 2014 in a variety of different cases and situations, and no case is the same. I'm not going to say that I've seen everything, but pretty close.

The most frequent unexpected problem I see is when someone has taken a plea that they really shouldn't have taken because the attorney that represented them on their criminal case didn't understand the immigration consequences that they would face and didn't advise them appropriately about the consequences of the plea they were taking.

Sometimes immigration judges or adjudication officers just get decisions wrong, and you have to appeal the decision. Immigration appeals can be complicated. Fortunately, they provide an opportunity for you to find the outcome you are looking for -- even after a denial.

CHAPTER 1

SOME OF THE MOST TROUBLING IMMIGRATION DECISIONS

The law around criminal convictions and the immigration consequences is complicated and always shifting. It's an area that immigration judges get wrong sometimes because the law is complicated, and they don't know the actual law and what convictions carry what immigration consequences.

There is something called the categorical approach which means that in the eyes of the immigration law you're only convicted of the minimum elements that a jury would have to find in order for you to be convicted of a crime and that may be less than what you did or less than what the title of the crime is. There's a lot of confusion. It is confusing for attorneys and judges to figure out what a conviction means for immigration purposes. So decisions in this area are often wrong and need to be challenged.

Difficulty For Immigrants Challenging Unlawful Or Unfair Decisions

It's not something I would recommend doing alone. If you were to handle it alone and got a bad decision, an appeal is a lot more complicated. Only about 5% of appeals are successful. It is something that you should explore if you're unhappy with the decision, especially if it's a deportation order that's going to mess up your life. But you do need to be ready for the fact that it's going to be an uphill battle.

Information Needed To Initiate A Case Against An Unlawful Or Unfair Immigration Decision

The most valuable thing you need is a copy of the full decision.

This way I can see why the judge made the decision, and I can start trying to look for ways to poke holes in it.

I will also need full details about your criminal history if I am going to handle your case. This is something that a lot of people are shy talking about but it's something you've got to get over because I can't help you if I don't know all the details. As your attorney, I'm here to help you and I need to know what the situation is that I'm facing.

The next thing I need is your immigration record. This information should include details such as:

- Whether you are here legally or illegally;
- What kind of visas or other statuses you have ever had;
- Whether there's ever been an accusation of fraud against you by the government;
- What country you're from;
- When you came to the United States;
- What family members do you have that are US citizens or permanent residents;

- Any special hardships that family members might suffer if you get deported;
- And more…

There is a lot of information I need to know. In the initial interview, I will be asking some probing questions that are a lot more detailed than you're used to talking to a stranger about, and maybe somewhat embarrassing. But I'm not asking these questions for fun. I need to know about it to know if I can help you and to know how to help you.

Potential Actions Taken To Challenge These Decisions

If you have a criminal record that is affecting your immigration situation, you will likely need to take extra steps to find a favorable review of your case.

A criminal record of any kind is going to be a negative discretionary factor and someone's going to look at it and be less likely to give you what you want. However, where it's only discretionary, requesting a new trial is not going to help because they're still going to be able to see that you were charged and make their own judgment.

The difference between a conviction and some other outcome matters more when it makes you eligible for deportation when you would not otherwise be deportable; makes you ineligible for relief from deportation, or makes you ineligible for some kind of status that you want to petition for.

Almost all drug crimes, many offenses involving violence or dishonesty, falsely claiming to be a US citizen, and certain firearm crimes have immigration consequences. There are a whole lot of different crimes that carry immigration consequences and some are less serious crimes than you would expect to have such serious consequences.

If you have any of those convictions and they are causing you problems, (or if you're about to apply for something and are worried they're going to cause you problems), then it's worthwhile to assess whether there was anything that makes the conviction illegal or unconstitutional.

The most common reason for vacating a plea would be if your attorney advised you poorly about immigration consequences or you were forced into a plea because they weren't ready for trial. If the case went to trial and you got convicted, an appeal will be more complicated.

Then I would need to review the whole trial record and there are a lot of things that could have gone wrong: the judge made an incorrect ruling, the judge gave the jury incorrect instructions, your attorney asked them to exclude a juror that had a bias or your attorney failed to ask the judge to do something they should have done, such as give the jury an instruction that would have helped your case or failed to present a viable defense when one was available. It is going to be case-specific on what's doable but there are options.

CHAPTER 2

THE IMPACT A CRIMINAL RECORD HAS ON SOMEONE'S IMMIGRATION STATUS

It depends on what the record is and what their status is. Several different categories of crimes can make you deportable - even if you're a permanent resident or even if you have some status that otherwise would allow you to stay here long-term. Certain kinds of crimes carry mandatory deportation and that is almost any kind of

- moderate or more serious drug crime, such as anything that involves distribution or possession with intent,
- crimes that are violent or dishonest such as murder, and any aggravated felony.

Many other crimes can be classified as aggravated felonies based on the length of your sentence. So that's something you need to look out for.

Sometimes, whether you got a sentence of a year versus under a year can make a big difference. And some crimes will make you ineligible to apply for a status that you otherwise would be eligible to apply for – even if they don't make you deportable directly, they may cause you to get deported because you lose the opportunity to apply for something you needed.

Immigrants Face Biases In Criminal Cases

In Boston, the juries and judges are usually pretty fair, but that's not true everywhere. I would say there may be more bias in places where there are fewer immigrants, and biases against people of color in places where there are fewer people of color.

The Grounds On Which Someone Can File An Appeal Or Request A New Trial

If you take a plea, the plea has to be knowing, voluntary and intelligent. If you take a plea not knowing and not voluntarily, it can make the plea illegal. One of the biggest reasons to take a plea not knowing is that you were not advised properly about immigration consequences.

In Massachusetts, your criminal defense attorney has an obligation to warn you about immigration consequences that may come from a conviction. It's not enough to just say crimes can have immigration consequences. There is also a warning the judge is required to give you, which is not as detailed, but if they didn't give the warning at all, then that could be a basis for a motion for a new trial.

If they didn't do that and you are facing immigration consequences because of the conviction, that would be a reason to file a motion for a new trial.

It's a little bit harder to win when your attorney misadvised you or didn't advise you, but that's a possibility. When you talk to me, you should tell me about anything that seems unfair about the process because it may or may not matter, but I'm the one with the experience to make that judgment, not you.

Those are the main things for a plea. A trial is very complicated because there are a million different things that could go wrong. There are a lot of different possibilities such as:

- Having a juror with a bias; (Especially if your attorney asked the judge to exclude that juror and the judge didn't.)
- It was obvious that your attorney should have asked the judge to exclude the juror, but failed to;
- The judge didn't give the jury instructions correctly about the relevant law;
- They've made an incorrect legal ruling; (Such as if the actions you were accused of could not legally be the crime that you were accused of, the judge should have dismissed the case.)
- Evidence wasn't suppressed that should have been suppressed;

- And more…

What Can Keep You From Removal Proceedings?

A full dismissal will keep you from removal proceedings based on the crime. It is important to understand what a dismissal means in this context.

Some forms of pleas have what's called a "continuance without finding" where you admit that the government could have convicted you of a crime if it had enough evidence, but you're choosing to take a plea instead of going to trial. Then you take probation, and the case is dismissed at the end of probation. [Other states have a similar process but have different names for it, such as a nolo contendere plea or an Alford plea].

This kind of disposition does not protect you from immigration consequences because any situation where you still have the admission of sufficient facts to make up a conviction and a punishment still counts as a conviction for immigration purposes. It has to be a real dismissal that does not involve any kind of plea.

So, the only things that would help you are a straight dismissal or something like pretrial probation where you don't admit guilt. They call it pretrial probation but most of the time it's just an agreement to stay out of trouble for a certain amount of time and then the case gets dismissed. That can be an option. There are some more complicated options that might work but you need to be very careful about them, such as a guilty file—this is a situation where you admit guilt but the judge agrees not to give you any punishment. This is not a conviction for immigration purposes, but even the slightest bit of punishment, such as paying court costs, would turn it into a conviction.

In conclusion, a dismissal might protect you but make sure you understand what they mean when they say dismissal.

CHAPTER 3

HABEAS CORPUS AS IT RELATES TO IMMIGRATION LAW

Habeas corpus is a request to be released from unlawful detention. Where this comes up in immigration law, is going to be irrelevant to most, but it might be relevant to your family or friends. It may be possible to challenge a decision in federal court by filing habeas corpus when someone has been denied bond or if they've been detained for an extended period of time.

Filing a Habeas Corpus Petition

Someone who is detained can file a Writ of Habeas Corpus. There is one additional possibility that if you have a federal criminal conviction, it can be challenged by habeas corpus if your regular appeal period has expired and immigration consequences are coming from that conviction. But the primary use of habeas corpus in immigration law is for people that are detained by ICE and have been detained for a lengthy period of time and continue to be detained even though there's no deportation scheduled.

One situation where I filed a habeas corpus case was when someone who was deported and was successful in a motion to reopen his case, should have been allowed to come back, and immigration should have been required to facilitate his return, but they were not doing that. That is another situation where it's possible to file habeas corpus.

Relief Available To An Immigrant If Successful With The Habeas Corpus Petition

The remedy would be that the judge would order ICE to release them. It's not a panacea, it doesn't affect the underlying deportation case, but it will get the person out of jail.

CHAPTER 4

THE ADMINISTRATIVE PROCEDURE ACT

The Administrative Procedure Act, also known as the APA, is a law that governs how the government must create regulations. This is the process that an agency must follow when creating regulations. If an agency creates a regulation without following the APA, then that regulation can be challenged based on a failure to follow the APA.

Types Of Immigration-Related Claims That Can Be Brought Under The APA

This would not be an argument that they got your specific case wrong. It has to be that the regulation itself was created incorrectly.

Typically, this happens when they've rushed something through, and didn't allow for appropriate public comments. It's not something that is going to be clear from the details of your case, but it's something that I may know about based on the specifics of how a particular regulation was created.

When and Where An APA Suit Is Filed

APA suits are filed in federal court when there is a violation of the APA in the creation of a rule.

The most common reason for this would be that there's a violation of the notice-and-comment requirements where the public has to be told about a proposed regulation and allowed to comment on it. If they were not given that, then it can be a basis for invalidating the rule.

Another basis can be that it's arbitrary and capricious, which is pretty difficult to prove because agencies do get a lot of deference from the courts. But if it's a crazy decision, then that is a basis for the regulation being invalidated. Another basis would be a regulation violating a law passed by Congress.

There can be an unreasonable delay in creating a regulation or taking action. A challenge to some of the delays with processing work permits is currently pending. That is unreasonable because everyone is facing long delays based on the government just not taking the work seriously enough.

Bringing An APA Suit

Anyone who is affected by an unlawful regulation can bring an APA suit.

Possible Defendants Named in An APA Suit

The government agency that created the regulation must be named as a Defendant. Sometimes there may be multiple defendants. The agency that created the regulations (and therefore violated the APA) is named as a defendant, along with other agencies involved in carrying it out. This comes up a lot in immigration because responsibilities are split between several different agencies across the Department of Homeland Security, Department of Justice, and Department of State.

Court Ordered Relief In An APA Suit

The court can invalidate any regulation that was created unlawfully. If that regulation is what's causing problems for your case, then that would solve whatever problem that regulation created.

To be clear, the court would not usually order the immigration authorities to grant you the specific thing that you're applying for, but if the regulation is the only thing standing in your way, then they would ultimately have to give it to you.

CHAPTER 5

ATTORNEY SKILLS AND QUALIFICATIONS NEEDED TO HANDLE IMMIGRATION CASES

Legally, any attorney admitted to practice in the appropriate court could take on an APA case. However, I would be careful and assess whether the person has the competence to do it as it's not a remedy that's going to be available in every case. It is something that's only going to be there when there is a defect in the process of creating a regulation.

The attorney is going to have to be someone knowledgeable about administrative law and how it's going to impact your case. It is possible that you could bring an APA challenge and win, but still, lose your case if the bad regulation is not the only thing that's standing between you and success.

I have a lot of experience handling very complex cases. I know the details of the law and am comfortable operating in a complex legal environment.

INDEX

NOTES

Made in the USA
Monee, IL
05 November 2026

67387953R00021